iNTERCOM

2000

Jennifer E. Bixby

HH Heinle & Heinle Publishers
A DIVISION OF WADSWORTH, INC.
Boston, Massachusetts 02116

WORKBOOK

Cover: The Graphics Studio/Gerry Rosentswieg

ISBN 0-8384-1814-7

10 9 8 7 6 5 4 3

Contents

Name _____   Date _____

| Unit 1 | What's in the News? |

Questions with *why* and reasons with *to + verb* (text, page 7)

A **What's the news?** Read the following news articles. Then answer the questions below.

SWIM TEAM BAKE SALE
The Winfield High School swim team is having a bake sale this Friday at City Hall. The team needs money to pay for its trip next month to Miami. They are going there to compete in a national swim meet. The bake sale will feature delicious cakes, pies, cookies, and breads.

Music Concert to Celebrate Valentine's Day
Get in the mood for Valentine's Day by listening to romantic love songs, traditional and new. The Winfield Chorus will present a concert to celebrate Valentine's Day next Tuesday at 7 PM. Admission is free and all are welcome.

College Night at Winfield High School
Many students attended College Night at Winfield High School to find out more about colleges in New York State. College representatives answered questions from parents and students and gave them brochures, catalogs, and applications.

BOY SCOUTS CLEAN UP PARK
Winfield Boy Scout Troop 12 finished a month-long project to clean up the city park. They began with picking up trash. Then they painted all the old trash cans to make them more attractive. The scouts fixed several benches to make them safe to sit on. In the spring, they will plant new flowers to beautify the park. Winfield residents will enjoy the "new" park.

| Example |
Why does the swim team need money? *To pay for its trip to Miami.*

1. Why is the swim team going to Miami? _____

2. Why is Tom Logan going to the bake sale? _____

3. Why is the Winfield Chorus having a concert? _____

4. Why did Cristina and Gino go to the concert? _____

5. Why did students attend College Night? _____

6. Why did the Boy Scouts paint the trash cans? _____

7. Why did the Boy Scouts fix the benches? _____

8. Why are the Boy Scouts going to plant new flowers? _____

Talking about the news *(text, page 8)*

B **What's the right word.** In each sentence, circle the correct word, the verb or noun form. The first one is an example.

1. Gino and Cristina just ((announced)/ announcement) their wedding.
2. At the airport there are about fifty flight (arrived / arrivals) every hour.
3. The U.S president Abraham Lincoln (was born / birth) in 1809.
4. Andy's birthday (celebrate / celebration) was a wonderful party with delicious food and great music.
5. The typical (engage / engagement) in the U.S. is for about one year.
6. My cousin will (get married / marriage) next year.
7. The wedding (receive / reception) will be at my aunt and uncle's house.
8. Tomas (scores / score) a goal in every soccer game.
9. Gino and Cristina are making many plans for their (wed / wedding).
10. The baseball team had many exciting (win / wins) this year.

C **What about you?** Answer these questions about yourself and people you know.

> | Example |
> When and where were you born?   *I was born October 2, 1975, in Miami, Florida.*

1. When and where were you born?
   _____

2. What do you usually do to celebrate your birthday?
   _____

3. Where did your parents (or you/your sister/brother) get married?
   _____

4. Do you know someone who got married recently? Who?
   _____

5. Do you like to go to weddings? Why?
   _____

6. What do people usually do at a wedding reception in your country?
   _____

Yes/no questions and answers *(text, page 9)*

D **Personal questions.** Answer the questions. In your answers, give additional information.

> | Example |
> Do you have a job?
> *No, I go to school.*   OR   *Yes, I do. I work at Wilson's Sports Shop.*

1. Do you have a job?
   _____

Name _____ Date _____

2. Did you have English class yesterday?

_____

3. Was your last English class difficult?

_____

4. Is your English teacher American?

_____

5. Do you enjoy studying English?

_____

6. Does your family watch the news on TV?

_____

7. Do you read the newspaper every day?

_____

8. Did you read the newspaper this morning?

_____

9. Do you like to read the sports section of the newspaper?

_____

10. Are you planning a trip soon?

_____

Result clauses with *so* (text, page 10)

E **What do you think?** Complete each sentence with an idea of your own.

> **Example**
> *I stayed up until 1:00 AM last night*, so I'm very tired today.

1. _____ , so I'm very tired today.

2. My sister got married last month, so _____ .

3. _____ , so I am studying English.

4. Carlos wants to relax this weekend, so _____ .

5. Linda had a fight with her boyfriend last night, so _____ .

6. Mr. and Mrs. Gomez don't like to eat in restaurants, so _____ .

7. I have a big test tomorrow, so _____ .

8. I want to travel to _____ , so _____ .

9. _____ , so he has to get up early.

10. _____ , so they have to practice hard.

Talking about family life *(text, page 12)*

F **Life in another country.** On page 12 in your text, you read "Life in the United States." In this exercise you will write about family life in another country. It can be your native country, or the country of your parents or a classmate. First, write answers to the questions below.

1. What country are you (your parents/classmate) from? _____

2. At what age do people usually get married? _____

3. How do a man and woman announce their engagement? _____

   _____

4. How long is the typical engagement? _____

5. Who arranges the wedding? _____

6. Who pays for the wedding? _____

7. What do people usually do during the reception? _____

   _____

8. Do the bride and groom go on a honeymoon? _____

9. What is a popular place for a honeymoon? _____

   _____

G **Write about it.** Use the information from exercise F to write a paragraph about marriages and weddings in another country. Include as many details as you can. Be sure to indent the first line of your paragraph.

_____

_____

_____

_____

_____

_____

_____

_____

_____

_____

_____

Name _____   Date _____

H **Class announcements.** This activity can be done individually or in small groups. Write an announcement to put up in your class. It can be about something that happened or something that is going to happen. Some topics are: engagement, marriage, birth, sports, special events. After you write the announcement, read it to a partner or to your classmates. Can they help you improve it? Rewrite the announcement to make it better. Then put up your announcement in your classroom.

NOTE: Newspaper writers keep these question words in mind when they write their articles: Who? What? When? Where? Why? Be sure your paragraph includes information to answer these questions.

First draft

_____

_____

_____

_____

_____

_____

_____

_____

_____

_____

Rewrite

_____

_____

_____

_____

_____

_____

_____

_____

_____

_____

Unit 2 Another Look at the News

Reading newspaper articles *(text, page 18)*

A Word forms. Complete the chart below with words you learned on page 18 of your text.

Verb	Noun
treasure	*treasure*
sculpt	_____
exhibit	_____
_____	donation
_____	acquisition
direct	_____

B What's the best word? Use words from exercise A to complete the sentences. When necessary, change the word from singular to plural, or to the correct verb tense.

> **Example**
>
> The museum recently *acquired* an important collection of early American paintings.

1. Admission to the museum is free, but visitors can make a _____ of one or two dollars.
2. The police officer _____ the traffic near the accident yesterday, and told drivers to take a different road.
3. The new _____ of African art was fantastic. It is at the museum until next month.
4. Mr. Thomas brought back several _____ from his trip to Mexico. He collects Mexican paintings, and he bought some very good ones during his trip.
5. Alice is quite an artist. She _____ large pieces from wood. Her _____ are beautiful, and several are in museums.

C On your own. Write your own sentences, using words from exercise A.

> **Example**
>
> *I treasure the necklace my grandmother gave me.*

1. _____

2. _____

3. _____

4. _____

5. _____

Name _____ Date _____

D **Announcements.** Read each announcement and fill in the charts with information.

1.
Library Hosts Local Writer

Central Library announces its first "Meet the Author" event of the fall. This will be a very special evening with Kathy Beckett, local author of "Cooking in New England." She will talk about her book and bring some traditional dishes to try. Admission is free. The talk is Tuesday, October 9, at 7:30 PM.

2.
Soccer Clinic at High School

There will be a soccer clinic for girls ages 12-15 to improve game skills. It will be this Saturday, October 6, from 9:00 to 3:30 at the high school soccer field. Coaches will direct intensive practice and a game in the afternoon. Players should call 648-4900 to sign up for the clinic. Players should bring lunch and something to drink. The cost is $5.00.

What: _____   What: _____

Who: _____   Why: _____

When: _____   When: _____

Where: _____   Where: _____

Cost: _____   Cost: _____

Reading newspaper ads *(text, page 19)*
Negative statements *(text, page 20)*

E **That's not right!** Read the ad below, and then correct the statements.

West Side Apartment. Large 3 bedroom, one bath. Sunny location, small yard. Washer, dryer on premises, utilities not included. One block from city bus and train lines. 30 minutes to downtown. Contact West Side Realtors, 699-5301.

Example
The apartment has four bedrooms. *No, it doesn't. It only has three bedrooms.*

1. It is a studio apartment. _____

2. It has two bathrooms. _____

3. The yard is large. _____

4. The utilities are included. _____

5. It is far from public transportation. _____

6. It has downtown convenience. _____

F **Captain Jack's.** Read the ad for Captain Jack's Restaurant and answer the questions. If the answer is *no*, give additional information as in exercise E.

Captain Jack's

Super Seafood at Reasonable Prices!

Lobster is Captain Jack's specialty!
Lobster dinner $15.95
Chef's seafood special $9.95
For steak lovers, delicious grilled steak! $13.95
Salad and dessert included
Free coffee

At the corner of Main Street and Washington Avenue, Downtown. High on the 20th floor, with an unbeatable view of the city. One block from the subway. Open every day, 11 AM -10 PM.

1. Is Captain Jack's expensive?

   _____

2. How much is the lobster dinner?

   _____

3. Is dessert included with the lobster dinner?

   _____

4. Is steak Captain Jack's specialty?

   _____

5. Do they have steak?

   _____

6. How much is the coffee?

   _____

7. Is Captain Jack's convenient to downtown?

   _____

8. Does it have an ocean view?

   _____

9. How far is it from the subway?

   _____

10. Is it open for breakfast?

   _____

Name _____ Date _____

Telling time with *past, after, to,* and *of* (text, page 21)

G **What time is it?** For each clock, give the time in two ways.

Example

It's ten past seven.
It's ten after seven.

1.

_____

_____

2.

_____

_____

3.

_____

_____

4.

_____

_____

5.

_____

_____

6.

_____

_____

7.

_____

_____

8.

_____

_____

9.

_____

_____

Questions with *What time...?* (text, page 22)

H **A radio schedule.** Read the radio schedule. Then write the missing question or answer.

WGGH 87.7 FM

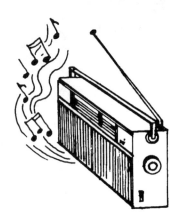

Monday - Thursday
5:00 A New Day (classical music)
7:00 Morning pro musica (classical and modern music)
12:00 Reading Aloud
12:30 Music America
4:30 All Things Considered (news)
6:00 Marketplace (business news)

> **Example**
>
> *What time is Reading Aloud on?*   It's on at 12:00.

1. What time is Marketplace on?   _____

2. _____   It's on at 5:00 AM.

3. What time is Morning pro musica on?   _____

4. _____   It's on at 12:30.

5. What time is All Things Considered on? _____

Questions with *How long...?* (text, page 22)

I **What's the schedule?** Use the cues to write a conversation. Use *How long* in the questions. Then write the answers, using information in the radio schedule.

> **Example**
>
> A New Day   A: *How long does A New Day last?*
>   B: *It lasts 2 hours.*

1. Morning pro musica   A: _____
                         B: _____

2. Reading Aloud   A: _____
                         B: _____

3. Music America   A: _____
                         B: _____

4. All Things Considered A: _____
                         B: _____

Name _____ Date _____

Learn to + verb; past tense of *become* (text, page 23)

J   **What did they learn how to do?** Match the cues in column A with the cues in column B, showing what each person became after learning how to do something. Write the letter in the blank. For **12** and **l**, write about yourself. Then write out each sentence.

A.

d 1. Tom / play soccer when he was seven
___ 2. Vinh / speak English in high school
___ 3. Yohannes / drive a car when he moved to the U.S.
___ 4. Sarah / use a computer in college
___ 5. Jose / play the guitar when he was young
___ 6. John / speak Spanish in Mexico
___ 7. Kate / cook from her father
___ 8. Roger / type very fast
___ 9. Paulo / make things with wood when he was young
___10. Martha / fix electrical things in school
___11. Joseph / drive a truck
___12. I _____

B.

a. carpenter
b. guitarist in a band
c. truck driver last year
d. outstanding soccer player
e. famous chef in New York City
f. electrician
g. excellent secretary
h. excellent college student
i. Spanish teacher in Chicago
j. taxi driver
k. programmer at the hospital
l. _____

1. *Tom learned how to play soccer when he was seven. He became an outstanding soccer* _____
   player. _____

2. _____
   _____

3. _____
   _____

4. _____
   _____

5. _____
   _____

6. _____
   _____

7. _____
   _____

8. _____
   _____

9. _____
   _____

10. _____
    _____

11. _____
    _____

12. _____
    _____

K Boston events. Read the weekend events listed below. Then complete the chart.

Bolshoi Ballet The Soviet Union's leading ballet company performs at the Wang Center Friday and Saturday nights at 8 PM. Tickets are $40 - $75. Telephone 931-2000.

Laughing Wild, a new comedy by Christopher Durang, will open at the Boston University Theater, Saturday evening at 8 PM. Tickets are $10.

At Great Woods, Mansfield. Rock group the Hudson Brothers performs Saturday and Sunday nights at 8:30 PM. Tickets are $12 - $17.

Fly Festival, Worcester Airport. Saturday and Sunday, 10 AM - 4 PM. Free admission. Airplane and helicopter rides, old planes, games, music, demonstrations.

Floating Regatta, Rowes Wharf, Boston Harbor. Sunday, 11 AM - 5 PM. Three boat races, boat rides, tours, clambake dinner. Admission: $8 adults, $5 children.

New England Aquarium, Central Wharf, Boston. Open 7 days a week, 9-5. Admission: $7 adults, $3 children 3-15. Special exhibit- "Rain Forest: Secret Spaces, Darkened Places."

Boston by Foot Tours, 77 North Washington Street, Boston. Each walk, adult $7, children $4. *Heart of the Freedom Trail* and *Beacon Hill* Monday through Saturday, 10 AM, 12 noon, and 2:30 PM.

Event	Day(s)	Time(s)	Place	Cost

L A trip to Boston. Imagine that you are spending two days in Boston. What would you like to do? Write out a plan.

> **Example**
>
> *On Saturday morning, I would like to see....*

_____

_____

_____

_____

_____

Name _____ Date _____

| Unit 3 | Someday I'll Be... |

Talking about the future with *will* (text, page 29)

A **What will you do?** Answer the following questions. If you are not sure what you will do, use *probably* in your answer.

> **Example**
> What time will you get up tomorrow morning?
> *I'll get up at 6:30.* OR *I'll probably get up at 6:30.*

1. What time will you get up tomorrow morning?
   _____

2. What will the weather be tomorrow?
   _____

3. What will you do tomorrow morning?
   _____

4. What time will you have lunch?
   _____

5. Where will you eat lunch?
   _____

6. What will you do in the afternoon?
   _____

7. Where and when will you have dinner?
   _____

8. What will you do after dinner?
   _____

B **Future plans.** Write paragraphs about your plans. Give as many details as possible. Your answers can be true or imagined plans.

1. What will you do next weekend?
   _____
   _____
   _____
   _____

2. What will you do next year?
   _____
   _____
   _____
   _____

C **Holiday plans.** What is the next big holiday for you? How will you celebrate? Give as many details as possible.

> *I will celebrate Thanksgiving in a few weeks. My family and I will go to my aunt and uncle's house in Chicago. We will probably leave on Wednesday night. The trip will take about 3 hours. On Thanksgiving, we will all...*

_____

_____

_____

_____

_____

_____

_____

Result clauses with *so* (text, page 30)

D **What's the result?** Use your imagination to write result clauses with *so* to complete these sentences.

> Example
>
> It's a beautiful warm day, *so I'll go to the beach with my friends.*

1. It's a beautiful warm day, _____

2. I have a big test tomorrow, _____

3. Miguel is studying very hard for the test, _____

4. Kim has a bad headache, _____

5. She took some aspirin, _____

6. Alice practices every day before her matches, _____

7. Tom wants to be a doctor, _____

8. The baby looks sick, _____

9. Marge has a new job as a flight attendant, _____

10. Tim's birthday is tomorrow, _____

Name _____ Date _____

Negative statements with *will* (text, page 31)

E **Not tomorrow!** Look at what each person was planning to do tomorrow. Unfortunately, the weather report predicts rain. Tell what each person won't do.

Example
The Browns *won't have their party outside.*

1. Manuel _____.

2. Ann and Judy _____.

3. The Smiths _____.

4. Andy _____.

5. Rifa and Karen _____.

6. Paolo _____.

7. Miguel _____.

8. Ed and May _____.

Talking about *astrology* *(text, page 32)*

F **Discussion questions.** First unscramble the astrology words. Then answer the questions. When you are finished, talk about your answers with a partner or in a group.

pocesohro _____   terufu _____   gins _____

latosoregr _____   trsa _____   kys _____

1. What is an astrologer?
   _____

2. What is your sign? (If you aren't sure, look on page 28 of your text.)
   _____

3. Do you ever read your horoscope? Why or why not?
   _____

4. Do you think people can predict the future?
   _____

5. Do you want someone to predict your future? Why or why not?
   _____

Irregular past tense *find (out), lose, meet, pay, read, sell, think, wake up* *(text, page 32)*

G **What did you do?** Write the past tense forms of these verbs. Then write five sentences about yourself, using past tense forms from the list.

find _____   lose _____   meet_____   pay _____
read _____   sell _____   think _____   wake up _____

1. _____
2. _____
3. _____
4. _____
5. _____

H **Past tense review.** Do you remember the past tense forms of these verbs from *Intercom 2000, Book 2*?

1. buy _____   5. win _____   9. fall _____   13. make _____

2. come_____   6. beat _____   10. break _____   14. do _____

3. lose _____   7. eat _____   11. hurt _____   15. leave _____

4. have _____   8. get _____   12. is _____   16. are _____

Questions and short answers with *will* (text, page 34)

Information questions with *will* (text, page 36)

I **A fantastic trip!** Imagine that you won two airline tickets to anywhere in the world. You also won money to stay in any hotel and to spend on your trip. You will go for one week. Where will you go and what will you do? Answer the questions, using *will*.

1. Where will you go on your trip?

   _____

2. Who will you invite to go with you?

   _____

3. Will this be your first time to the country?

   _____

4. Will you visit any friends or relatives there?

   _____

5. Will you go to big cities? Which ones?

   _____

6. What will you see on your trip?

   _____

7. What souvenirs will you buy?

   _____

8. Will you take any small trips to the countryside?

   _____

J **Thinking about your future.** Answer the following questions about your future. Give as many details as possible.

1. What will you be doing in 20 years?

   _____

   _____

   _____

   _____

2. Where will you be living? Who will you be living with?

   _____

   _____

   _____

   _____

K **Fifty years from now.** Answer the questions below. Then in small groups or pairs, share your answers. Talk about similarities and differences in your answers.

1. How will you be different in fifty years? What will you be doing? How will you be the same? What will your life be like?

_____

_____

_____

_____

_____

_____

_____

_____

_____

_____

2. How will the world be different? How will it be the same?

_____

_____

_____

_____

_____

_____

_____

_____

_____

_____

Name _____   Date _____

Unit 4 | **Fire at the Plaza** |

Talking about a fire *(text, page 40)*

A **Scrambled story.** The sentences below tell the story of a fire in the Windshire Apartment Building. Number the sentences and then write them in the correct order in the paragraph below. (Note: resident = someone who lives in a place)

_____ a. The firefighters told them not to jump but to wait for the ladder.

_____ b. The fire was under control by 11:15 PM.

_____ c. The fire department arrived at 10:40 PM, and found the first floor full of smoke and fire.

_____ d. A resident found the fire at 10:30 PM, and called the fire department.

_1.__ e. The fire started on the first floor in the front bedroom.

_____ f. The residents were yelling for help from the windows when they arrived.

_____ g. Then she ran to the second and third floors and yelled to wake up the other residents.

_____ h. They rescued the residents quickly and safely with the ladders.

　　　Four fire trucks responded to a serious fire at the Windshire Apartment Building on South Street yesterday. *The fire started on the first floor in the front bedroom.*

_____

_____

_____

_____

_____

_____

_____

_____

One firefighter had a slight injury and was taken by ambulance to the hospital.

Talking about past events with *there was* and *there were* (text, page 40)

B **The fire at the Windshire.** Write statements about the story in exercise A using *there was* and *there were*.

> **Example**
>
> serious fire / Windshire Apartment Building
> *There was a serious fire at the Windshire Apartment Building.*

1. four fire trucks / at the fire

   _____

2. fire / first floor

   _____

3. several residents / building

   _____

4. one slight injury

   _____

5. an ambulance / at the scene of the fire

   _____

6. two ladders / at the windows

   _____

7. a lot of smoke / from the fire

   _____

8. several police cars / in the street

   _____

Name _____   Date _____

Questions and short answers with *there was* and *there were* (text, page 42)

C **School announcements.** Read last week's school announcements. Then write questions and answers, using the words given. For numbers 8, 9, and 10, make up your own questions and answers.

SCHOOL ANNOUNCEMENTS

SPANISH CLUB MEETING: Wednesday, 7 PM. Bake Sale, Friday
NEWSPAPER MEETING: Monday, 7 PM
STUDENT ACTION COMMITTEE MEETING: Wednesday, 6:30 PM. Bake Sale, Thursday
GIRLS' SOCCER GAMES: Monday and Wednesday, 4:00
BOYS' SOCCER GAMES: Tuesday and Thursday, 4:00
FOOTBALL PRACTICE: Monday and Thursday, 4:00
FOOTBALL GAME AGAINST CENTRAL HIGH: Friday, 7 PM

Example

football practice / Friday
A: *Was there football practice on Friday?*
B: *No, there wasn't.*

---

1. football game / Friday night

A: _____

B: _____

2. newspaper meeting / Monday afternoon

A: _____

B: _____

3. two girls' soccer games / last week

A: _____

B: _____

4. boys' soccer game / Friday

A: _____

B: _____

5. two bake sales / last week

A: _____

B: _____

6. Spanish Club meeting / Wednesday night

A: _____

B: _____

7. bake sale / Monday

A: _____

B: _____

8.

A: _____

B: _____

9.

A: _____

B: _____

10.

A: _____

B: _____

Talking about past events: past continuous statements *(text, page 44)*

D **Create a story.** Imagine that you were shopping at a mall yesterday. There was a fire. Complete the sentences below, creating your own story. Here are some verbs you can use: *yell, direct, help, look, shop, run, walk, watch, arrive, put out (a fire), burn, stand.* You may use some words more than once.

> **Example**
>
> Yesterday afternoon, *I was shopping for new shoes at the mall.*

1. Yesterday afternoon, I _____ .

2. Many people _____ and the stores were full.

3. Suddenly, I heard the fire alarm. Everyone had to leave the buildings. Salespeople

   _____ .

4. Some people _____ , but most

   people _____ .

5. In a few minutes, the fire trucks arrived. Some firefighters _____

   _____ . Others _____ .

6. The fire _____ in the _____ . It wasn't a big fire, but it was

   very smoky.

7. I _____ in a crowd of people outside the mall, and we

   _____ the fire when the police told us to move back.

Asking about past events: past continuous questions *(text, page 45)*

E **What were you doing?** Answer the questions, giving additional information when possible.

> **Example**
>
> Were you sitting in English class yesterday morning?
> *No, I wasn't. I was reading in the library.*

1. Were you sitting in English class yesterday morning?

   _____

2. Were you eating lunch at 12:00 yesterday? If not, when were you eating lunch?

   _____

3. Who were you eating with?

   _____

4. What were you doing yesterday at 4:00 in the afternoon?

   _____

Name _____ Date _____

5. Where were you doing this?

_____

6. Were you studying English last night?

_____

7. Were you talking on the phone last night? If so, who were you talking to?

_____

8. What were you watching on TV last night?

_____

9. What were you and your friends talking about before class today?

_____

10. Were you talking in English?

_____

Past continuous statements; clauses with *when* (text, page 46)

F   **What was happening?** Write about the pictures. Use the cues to write sentences.

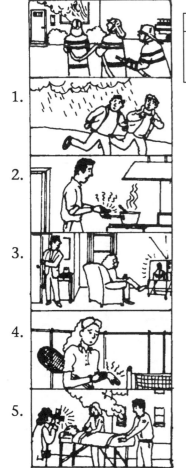

Example
come from / arrive *Smoke was coming from the windows when the firefighters arrived.*

1. run / start to rain

_____

_____

2. cook / burn his hand

_____

3. watch TV / father come home

_____

_____

4. play tennis /hurt wrist

_____

_____

5. help an injured person / photographer take a picture

_____

Interrupted actions vs. continuous actions *(text, page 47)*

G **The party.** Look at the picture of the party. Answer the questions, using complete sentences with either the past continuous or the simple past.

> **Example**
>
> What happened while Alan was cooking hamburgers?
> *While Alan was cooking hamburgers, he dropped one.*

1. What was he doing while he was cooking hamburgers?

   _____

2. What happened when the kids were playing volleyball?

   _____

3. What was one boy doing while the kids were playing volleyball?

   _____

4. What happened while he was climbing the tree?

   _____

5. What was Sally doing when Roger invited her to dance?

   _____

6. What was Vinh doing when the dog took his hamburger?

   _____

7. What happened while Kim was sitting in the chair?

   _____

8. What happened to the watermelon when Alice was cutting it?

   _____

Name _____   Date _____

Disagreeing *(text, pages 48-49)*

H "You don't …" In each conversation below, a person disagrees and gives an example of when he or she *does* do something. Use the cues to complete the conversations.

Example
(last week)   MOTHER: You never clean your room!   SON: *But I do clean it. I cleaned it last week.*

1. (Wednesday)

DIANA: You never call me during the week.

ROBIN: _____

2. (two pieces / this afternoon)

HUSBAND: You don't like my cake.

WIFE: _____

3. (day before yesterday)

MIGUEL: You don't have lunch with me very often.

AL: _____

4. (last night)

BECKY: You never wash your dishes.

ROSA: _____

5. (every day this week)

BOSS: You never start work on time.

EMPLOYEE: _____

Final Activity

I **Bee in truck causes accident.** Read the newspaper article. Then answer the questions in complete sentences.

Useful vocabulary:

bee = a flying bug that gives a painful sting

cab (of a truck) = the area where the driver sits

median strip = an area between the two directions of traffic, usually grassy

tip over = fall over

swat = hit

unable = not able

BEE IN TRUCK CAUSES ACCIDENT

WESTFIELD — An ambulance took two men to Emerson Hospital after a truck crossed over the median strip on Route 12, tipped over on its side, and was hit by an oncoming car last Thursday evening.

Frank Watson, 36, from Bradford, was swatting a bee that entered the cab of his truck when he crossed into the oncoming traffic. The truck was carrying computer equipment from Bradford to Southboro when it tipped on its side. It blocked two lanes of traffic, said State Police Officer Mark Wilson.

Michael Stone, 37, from Fitchburg, was unable to stop. The car drove through the roof of the truck, said Wilson. Both Stone and Watson had minor injuries. The ambulance took them to Emerson Hospital and they were able to go home that evening.

1. How many vehicles (cars / trucks) were in the accident?

   _____

2. Were there any injuries?

   _____

3. Was there a fire?

   _____

4. Where was the truck driver driving from?

   _____

5. What was the truck carrying?

   _____

6. What was the truck driver doing when he crossed the median strip?

   _____

7. How old was the driver of the car?

   _____

8. What did the car do?

   _____

9. Which hospital did the two injured men go to?

   _____

10. When did they leave the hospital?

   _____

Name _____ Date _____

Unit 5 — Look At These Headlines!

Talking about crime; irregular past tense: *steal, catch* (text, page 54)

A **A newspaper report.** Below are a newspaper reporter's notes about a robbery. Read the notes and then write out the story.

> *Quick Stop Convenient Store, N. Main Street.*
> *12 midnight, Wed. night.*
> *Closing time.*
> *Robbers entered while clerk closing store.*
> *2 men — both around 25.*
> *Took about $500.*
> *No injuries.*
> *Escaped in black sports car.*
> *Clerk called police immediately.*
> *Arrived 12:20 - didn't catch robbers.*
> *Crime under investigation.*

_____

_____

_____

_____

_____

_____

_____

Reading news headlines *(text, page 55)*

B **Understanding headlines.** Write a sentence to describe each headline. For reference, see Presentation, page 55, in your text.

> **Example**
>
> PRESIDENT TO VISIT MEXICO NEXT MONTH
> *The President will visit Mexico next month.*

1. ITALY WINS SOCCER MATCH

   _____

2. POLICE CATCH LAWYER WITH STOLEN PAINTING

   _____

3. LIBRARY TO START EVENING MOVIE SERIES

   _____

4. SNOW CONTINUING ON EAST COAST

   _____

5. MUSEUM GETS MONEY FOR NEW BUILDING

   _____

6. SCHOOLS TO START WINTER VACATION NEXT WEEK

   _____

7. NEW POOL TO OPEN IN SUMMER

   _____

8. AMERICANS EXERCISING MORE THAN 10 YEARS AGO

   _____

9. BOY FINDS 100-YEAR-OLD TREASURES IN YARD

   _____

10. GIRLS' TENNIS TEAM WINNING EVERY MATCH

    _____

C **What are the headlines?** Write headlines about events in your class or school or news about your classmates. Work in pairs or small groups if possible.

> **Examples**
>
> *TEACHER SICK ON MONDAY*
> *TEST TO BE ON FRIDAY*
> *STUDENTS PLANNING CLASS PARTY*

1. _____

2. _____

3. _____

4. _____

5. _____

Name _____ Date _____

Position of adverbs of frequency with verbs *(text, page 57)*

D **What about you?** Read the chart and check how often *you* read different sections of the newspaper.

DO YOU READ...	Always	Usually	Often	Sometimes	Rarely	Never
Headlines						
Sports						
International News						
Local News						
TV Guide						
Arts						
Movie Guide						
Letters to the Editor						
Horoscope						
Advice Column						
Comics						
Science News						
Garden News						
Classified Ads						
Births & Deaths						

E **Write about yourself.** Use information from the chart above to write sentences about how often you read different sections of the newspaper and why. Give some additional information with each sentence.

> **Example**
>
> *I always read the headlines because I want to know the most important stories.*
> *I never read sports because I think sports are boring.*

1. _____

2. _____

3. _____

4. _____

5. _____

6. _____

7. _____

8. _____

9. _____

10. _____

And so + do/does/did + noun *(text, page 58)*

F **Interview.** Ask your classmates the questions below, and try to find two people to answer *yes* to each question. One of those persons can be yourself. For numbers 9 and 10, write your own questions.

	YES	
	1.	2.

1. Do you speak English? _____ _____

2. Do you drink tea in the morning? _____ _____

3. Did you drink tea this morning? _____ _____

4. Do you always watch the news on TV? _____ _____

5. Do you have to do chores on the weekend? _____ _____

6. Did you stay up late last night? _____ _____

7. Did you study yesterday? _____ _____

8. Do you like horror movies? _____ _____

9. Do you _____? _____ _____

10. Did you _____? _____ _____

G **What did you find out?** Now write statements about each question from exercise F.

Example
I speak English, and so does Marie.   *Sonya drank tea this morning, and so did Minh.*

1. _____

2. _____

3. _____

4. _____

5. _____

6. _____

7. _____

8. _____

9. _____

10. _____

It's + adjective + to + verb (text, page 59)

H   **What do you think?** Write sentences using *it's* + each of the following adjectives: *great, impossible, good, sad, possible, wonderful, expensive, boring, hard, important, dumb, nice.* You will not use every adjective.

> **Example**
>
> *It's great to have two weeks of vacation.*

1. _____
2. _____
3. _____
4. _____
5. _____
6. _____
7. _____
8. _____
9. _____
10. _____

Indefinite pronouns *something, anything, nothing* (text, page 59)

I   **Which pronoun?** Complete the sentences with *anything, something, nothing.*

1. A: Did you buy <u>*anything*</u> at the mall?
   B: No, I didn't buy _____ .
2. A: Are you planning _____ for your next vacation?
   B: I don't have _____ planned yet, but I'm sure I'll do _____ .
3. _____ is wrong with my car, so I have to take it to the mechanic.
4. A: What was that crash? Did _____ break?
   B: No, _____ broke.
5. A: Do you want _____ to drink?
   B: No, _____ for me right now, thanks.
6. There's _____ good at the movie theater, so we won't go this week.
7. A: Did you do _____ exciting last night?
   B: Not really. We just went out for _____ to eat.
8. There wasn't _____ to do, so the workers went home.
9. A: What happened?
   B: _____ .
10. I have to make _____ for the party. Maybe I'll make a big salad.

Irregular plurals *(text, page 61)*

J **Watch your spelling!** Fill in the blanks with the missing singular or plural form of the noun.

1.	leaf	*leaves*	8.	roof	_____		
2.	chief	_____	9.	_____	wives		
3.	_____	scarves	10.	woman	_____		
4.	man	_____	11.	knife	_____		
5.	_____	beliefs	12.	_____	chefs		
6.	loaf	_____	13.	thief	_____		
7.	_____	children	14.	_____	wolves		

K **Make a sentence.** Use the cues to write sentences. Change the nouns that have irregular plurals to the plural form. (See exercise J.) Put the verb in the past tense. (Note: In 6, *tribe* is a group of people living under a leader or chief.)

> **Example**
> child / buy / loaf
> *The children bought three loaves of bread at the store yesterday.*

1. chef / prepare a wonderful meal

   _____

2. man and woman / play volleyball / beach

   _____

3. child / play / leaf / in the fall

   _____

4. man / buy scarf / wife

   _____

5. snow / cover the roof / during snowstorm

   _____

6. Native American chief / have meeting / tribe

   _____

7. thief / carry/ knife

   _____

8. wolf / catch small animals to eat

   _____

Name _____   Date _____

L **A letter to the editor.** Read the newspaper article below. Then write a letter of opinion to the editor of the newspaper. You can take the role of a student, parent, teacher, coach, or librarian. In your letter, be sure to tell who you are, what you are writing about, and give your opinion. Support your opinion with examples and give possible solutions to the problem. When you have finished your letter, share it with a classmate. Can he or she make any suggestions for improving your letter?

Useful expressions:
I think it is important / bad / sad / impossible / expensive...
I think we should ...
In my opinion, ...

NO MONEY FOR AFTER-SCHOOL SPORTS, MUSIC

The high school school superintendent announced yesterday that there is no money this year for after-school sports or music. He said that this year the school needs to buy many new books and encyclopedias for the school library. Last year there was no money for new books, and the teachers complained that the library books were out of date and there were not enough encyclopedias. The superintendent is calling this year the Year of the Book, and is encouraging students and parents to support the library renewal effort.

Meanwhile, school coaches, the band leader, and orchestra instructor are very upset about the new situation. Coach Wilson said, "This happens every few years. No one manages the money well, and so there isn't enough for all programs. There *is* enough money, but the superintendent just needs to learn how to spend it more wisely and fairly. There are so many kids that enjoy these after-school activities." The superintendent is setting up a committee to help raise money through bake sales, car washes, etc. Most teachers will be happy to see new books in the library, but agree that after-school activities are important.

_____

_____

_____

_____

_____

_____

_____

_____

_____

_____

_____

Unit 6 **At the Dentist's Office**

Talking about a visit to the dentist *(text, page 66)*

A **All about teeth.** Use the vocabulary below to complete the sentences. You will use some words more than once.

Vocabulary: appointment / brush / cavity / checkup / clean / dentist / gums / hurt / patient(s) / pull / take care of / teeth / toothache

1. A _____ is a doctor who _____ your teeth and _____ .

2. People usually visit the _____ twice a year for a _____ .

3. During a _____ , the _____ checks the _____'s _____ and _____ .

4. Dentists usually tell their _____ to _____ their teeth twice a day to keep them _____ and healthy.

5. Dentists don't like to _____ their patients _____ , but sometimes they have to fill a _____ in a tooth.

6. If a tooth is very bad, the dentist has to _____ the tooth.

7. If you have a bad _____ , you should make an _____ with your _____ .

Inseparable two-word verbs *(text, page 66)*

B **At the doctor.** Complete the conversation using the verbs listed. Use each verb only once and change the verb forms as needed.

call / come back / come in / feel / give / have / look at / look for / take / talk with / sit down

Useful vocabulary:
antibiotic = a medicine used to treat infection
medical record = a written medical history of a patient, including notes about visits, checkups, etc.
strep throat = a bacterial infection in the throat
swollen = when something gets larger, increases in size
throat culture = a sample of throat bacteria that is taken to test for infection

Name _____ Date _____

Alex is sitting in the waiting room at a clinic.
He has a bad sore throat and a fever.
He is waiting for his appointment with
the doctor.

DR. MENDES: Alex Green?
ALEX: Yes.
DR. MENDES: Hi, Alex. Please (1) _____ . So, you aren't (2) _____ very
             well?
ALEX: No. Actually I feel terrible. I got this sore throat and fever two days ago, and
             I (3) _____ to stay home from work yesterday.
DR. MENDES: I see. Just a minute while I (4) _____ your medical record.
             Oh, here it is. Please (5) _____ in this chair and let me
             (6) _____ your throat. Yes, it looks very red and swollen.
             I want to take your temperature too.
ALEX: Do I still have a fever?
DR. MENDES: Yes, it's about 102. I'm going to take a throat culture to see if you have
             strep throat. Please (7) _____ the office tomorrow afternoon
             and (8) _____ the nurse about the culture results.
ALEX: Do I need to (9) _____ to see you again?
DR. MENDES: Probably not. If it is strep throat, the nurse will (10) _____ you
             instructions, and will call the drugstore with a prescription. The antibiotics
             will (11) _____ care of the infection. If it isn't strep throat, it is
             probably the flu and you should be better in a few days. Just take it easy,
             stay home from work until you feel better, and get plenty of rest.
ALEX: Thanks, Dr. Mendes.
DR. MENDES: You're welcome. Bye.
ALEX: Good-bye.

C **Questions about his visit.** Write complete answers to the questions about Alex's visit
to the doctor.

1. What's wrong with Alex?

    _____

2. What did Dr. Mendes have to look for at first?

    _____

3. Did Dr. Mendes look at Alex's throat? How was it?

    _____

4. When does Alex have to call back?

    _____

5. Who will he talk with?

    _____

Giving reasons *(text, page 68)*

D **Give the reasons.** Complete each sentence with *because...* Use your imagination.

> **Example**
>
> Kim is at home today *because she has a bad sore throat.*

1. Toshio is at home today _____

_____ .

2. They have to take the car to the mechanic _____

_____ .

3. I have to go to the post office _____

_____ .

4. The driver was in a terrible accident _____

_____ .

5. My friend was in the hospital last week _____

_____ .

6. My aunt and uncle go back to Florida every year for vacation _____

_____ .

7. Leona is studying computer programming_____

_____ .

8. Mike didn't finish his homework _____

_____ .

9. Kim didn't study for the test _____

_____ .

10. Jean isn't talking to her boyfriend _____

_____ .

E **Decisions.** Did you decide something recently? Tell what you decided and why. It can be an important decision or a small decision.

> **Example**
>
> *I decided to exercise more because I am out of shape.*
> *I decided to invite my girlfriend to my house because I want her to meet my parents.*

1. _____

_____

2. _____

_____

3. _____

_____

Name _____ Date _____

F **Why are you studying English?** Write about why you are studying English. Give several reasons with *because*.

> | Example |
>
> *I am studying English because I live in the U.S. now.*
> *I need to speak English because I want to travel to the U.S.*

_____

_____

_____

_____

_____

_____

Position of adverbs of frequency
(text, page 70)

G What kind of English student are you? Look at the chart below and check the right boxes about yourself.

What kind of English student are you?	Always	Usually	Rarely	Never
1. I arrive on time to class.				
2. I speak my native language in class.				
3. I give correct answers to questions.				
4. I can correct my own mistakes.				
5. I help classmates with their English.				
6. I forget to do my homework.				
7. I ask the teacher questions.				
8. I study English every day.				
9. I think in English.				
10. I enjoy studying English.				

H **Write about yourself.** Use information from the chart in exercise G to write sentences about yourself as an English student. For 11 and 12, add two sentences of your own.

> **Example**
>
> 1. *I usually arrive on time to class.*
> 11. *I always listen to music while I am studying English at home.*

1. _____
2. _____
3. _____
4. _____
5. _____
6. _____
7. _____
8. _____
9. _____
10. _____
11. _____
12. _____

I **Ask a partner.** Use cues from the chart in exercise G to write five questions to ask your partner. You can also make up some of your own questions. Then write your partner's answers.

> **Example**
>
> A: *Do you study English every day?*
> B: *Yes, I usually study English every day.*

1. A: _____?
   B: _____
2. A: _____?
   B: _____
3. A: _____?
   B: _____
4. A: _____?
   B: _____
5. A: _____?
   B: _____

Name _____ Date _____

If-clauses with present tense verbs, *can*, and *should* *(text, page 72)*

J **What do you do if . . . ?** Answer each question, telling what usually happens. Use *if*-clauses with present tense verbs and *can*.

> **Example**
> What do you usually do if you can't sleep?
> *If I can't sleep, I usually read a boring book.*

1. What do you usually do if you can't sleep?
   _____

2. What do you do if you have a bad cold?
   _____

3. What do you do if you need some exercise?
   _____

4. What do you do if you want to relax?
   _____

5. Who can you usually talk to if you have a serious problem?
   _____

6. What do you do if you are bored?
   _____

7. What can you do if you don't understand something in class?
   _____

8. Where do you go if you want to eat at a nice restaurant?
   _____

9. Where can you go if you want to take a walk?
   _____

10. Where do you go if you need to shop for clothes?
    _____

K **What's possible?** Finish each sentence, telling what is possible. Use *if*-clauses with *can* or *can't*.

> **Example**
> If it's sunny tomorrow, *we can go to the beach.*

1. If it's sunny tomorrow, _____.

2. If it rains tomorrow, _____.

3. If I make a lot of money this year, _____.

4. If you speak English very well, _____.

5. If I get sick tomorrow, _____.

L **What's your advice?** Finish each sentence, giving advice and using an *if*-clause with *should*.

> **Example**
>
> If you want to go to an expensive restaurant, *you should go to Chez Claude.*

1. If you want to go to an expensive restaurant, _____ .

2. If you want to speak English well, _____ .

3. If you want to read a good book, _____ .

4. If you like exciting movies, _____ .

5. If you want to get a lot of exercise, _____ .

6. If you want to go to a beautiful beach, _____ .

7. If you want to find a quiet place to read, _____ .

8. If you want to watch a great TV show, _____ .

Final Activity

M **A trip to the dentist.** Write a paragraph about a trip to the dentist. This can be your own dental visit or an imagined one. Give as many details as you can. For example: When did you go? Was it for a checkup, a cavity, or a toothache? Who did you see? What did he or she do? What did he or she tell you? Did it hurt?

Useful vocabulary:
dental floss = string that is pulled between the teeth to clean them
dental hygienist = the person who cleans people's teeth during the checkup
fill a cavity = to take out the bad part of a tooth and fill the hole with a hard material
receptionist = the person who greets patients and makes appointments
x-ray = a picture taken of teeth

_____

_____

_____

_____

_____

_____

_____

Name _____ Date _____

A Weight Problem?

Talking about weight *(text, page 79)*

A **Questions about Cristina.** Read the conversation on page 77 of your text again. Then answer the questions about Cristina's "weight problem." Answer in complete sentences.

> **Example**
>
> How much does Cristina weigh?
> *She weighs 115 pounds.*

1. What is Cristina's weight? _____

2. How tall is she? _____

3. What is Cristina's height? _____

4. What kind of frame does Cristina have? _____

5. Why does she want to go on a diet? _____

6. Does she feel healthy? _____

7. Does Doctor Young think Cristina should lose weight? Why not? _____

   _____

8. Does she need to gain weight? _____

9. What does Doctor Young suggest? _____

10. Does Dr. Young put Cristina on a diet? _____

B **Good health.** Use the vocabulary to complete the sentences. You will use some words several times.

Vocabulary: diet / frame / go on a diet / healthy / heavy / height / weigh / weight

Everyone wants to look and feel (1)_____ , but sometimes it is hard to know how. It is not just a matter of how much you (2)_____ — (3)_____ and (4)_____ size are also important. There is no perfect weight for a certain (5)_____ . A good (6)_____ depends on what type of (7)_____ you have: small, medium, or large. If you are too (8)_____ for your (9)_____ and (10)_____ type, you will need to (11)_____ to lose (12)_____ . In addition to following a diet, you will need to look at your exercise habits. Exercise and (13)_____ are both important for a (14)_____ body.

Prepositions of time: *in* and *for* (text, page 80)

C **Questions about time.** Answer the questions about yourself, using *in* or *for* in your answers.

> **Example**
>
> When are you going on vacation?
> *I am going on vacation in two weeks.*

1. When are you going on vacation?
   _____

2. Think about the last time you were sick. How long were you sick?
   _____

3. When are you going to be finished with this exercise?
   _____

4. How long do you study each night?
   _____

5. When is this year going to end? (Give the number of months or days until Jan. 1.)
   _____

6. How long would you like to exercise every day?
   _____

7. When is the next national holiday?
   _____

8. When is your birthday?
   _____

9. How long do you usually sleep at night?
   _____

Prepositions *(text, page 81)*

D **Getting into shape.** Complete the paragraph with *after / at / for / in / to / until / on.* You will use some words more than once.

(1)_____ his last medical checkup, Ahmed decided to get into better shape. First he needed to lose some weight. He went (2)_____ a diet (3)_____ two weeks. He lost seven pounds, and he felt better. He also started to exercise. Every morning (4)_____ 7:00, he went (5)_____ the swimming pool. He swam (6)_____ about half an hour. Then he took a shower, got dressed, and walked (7)_____ the bus stop. (8)_____ work, he had fruit, coffee, and a piece of toast for breakfast. Ahmed worked (9)_____ 12:30, and then he went to lunch (10)_____ the company cafeteria. He usually ate a salad and soup (11)_____ lunch. This routine made it easy to follow his diet and exercise plan. (12)_____ weekends, he rode his bike (13)_____ about an hour each day. He usually rode (14)_____ the park or (15)_____ the river.

Name _____ Date _____

More adjectives *(text, page 81)*

E **Adjective review.** Match each adjective in column A with its antonym (opposite) in column B. Write the letter in the blank.

A	B
____ 1. fat	a. loud
____ 2. impossible	b. easy
____ 3. important	c. healthy
____ 4. sad	d. possible
____ 5. boring	e. calm
____ 6. hard	f. thin
____ 7. sick	g. energetic
____ 8. violent	h. happy
____ 9. quiet	i. unimportant
____ 10. lazy	j. interesting

F **What's your opinion?** Give your opinion about five things. For example, about music, movies, places, people, books, etc. Use the adjectives in exercise E.

> **Example**
>
> *I think Sam is a very energetic person.*

1. _____

2. _____

3. _____

4. _____

5. _____

G **What's the best word?** Read each item and circle the correct word.

> **Example**
>
> I didn't sleep much last night so, I feel very (lazy / easy) today.

1. Cake and ice cream are very (big / fattening) foods.

2. The math test is going to be very (hard / unimportant), so I am going to study for it tonight.

3. That movie isn't very (violent / happy). No one is badly injured or hurt.

4. It is too (quiet / loud) in that cafeteria. It's hard to have a conversation.

5. She didn't buy the dress because it was too (thin / expensive). She didn't have enough money.

Giving excuses or reasons *(text, page 82)*

H Excuses. Answer the questions using the cues given.

> **Example**
>
> Why doesn't she come with us? (tired)
> *Maybe she's too tired to come with us.*

1. Why doesn't he clean his room? (lazy)
   _____

2. Why don't the children sit quietly? (energetic)
   _____

3. Why doesn't she sing with her school group? (shy)
   _____

4. Why doesn't he buy his girlfriend a present? (broke)
   _____

5. Why doesn't she help her sister? (selfish)
   _____

6. Why don't the boys relax before the soccer game? (nervous)
   _____

7. Why doesn't she stop crying? (upset)
   _____

8. Why doesn't he carry the box himself? (heavy)
   _____

9. Why doesn't she eat the dessert? (fattening)
   _____

10. Why doesn't he want to see that movie? (violent)
    _____

Every, every other (text, page 83)

I How often? Complete the sentences with *every* or *every other*.

1. She exercises on Monday, Wednesday, and Friday. She exercises _____ day.
2. On his new exercise plan, he walks _____ day, Monday through Sunday.
3. The Smiths always celebrate Mr. Smith's birthday with a big party. They have a party _____ year.
4. The college student told his parents not to call him every week.   Now they just call _____ week.
5. The Nortons go out to dinner often.   In fact, they go out _____ weekend.
6. My cousin is very interested in historical museums. Last year he went to _____ historical museum in San Francisco.
7. During the summer I played tennis every weekend. Now I'm too busy, so I only play _____ weekend.
8. She watches the late night news on TV _____ night before she goes to bed.

Future conditional clauses with *if* (text, page 84)

J **What will happen?** Answer the questions with complete sentences.

> **Example**
>
> What will happen if you drink too much coffee?
> *If I drink too much coffee, I won't sleep well.*

1. What will happen if you stay up too late?

   _____

2. What will happen if you eat too much?

   _____

3. What will happen if you don't exercise or eat well?

   _____

4. What will happen if you don't study your English?

   _____

5. What will happen if you wake up late?

   _____

6. What will happen if you don't brush your teeth?

   _____

7. What will happen if you lift something that is too heavy?

   _____

8. What will happen if you go outside without a jacket when it's very cold?

   _____

All (of), some of, none of (text, page 85)

K **Describe the picture.** Look at the picture and describe what was happening when the picture was taken. Use *all (of), some of, none of* and *was/were +* verb *+ -ing.* Here are some verbs you can use: *talk / wear / stand / make / cut / wash / eat.*

Making pizza at Jose's.

When this picture was taken, _____

_____

_____

_____

_____

Too + adjective + for + object (text, page 87)

L Why not? Write reasons for each statement, using the cues given.

> **Example**
>
> I'm not going to play tennis. (windy)
> *It's too windy for me to play tennis.*

1. Tom isn't going on vacation this year. (expensive)
    _____

2. They can't stay out longer tonight. (late)
    _____

3. I don't want to eat that cake. (fattening)
    _____

4. They don't like to study in that room. (noisy)
    _____

5. He can't carry that box. (heavy)
    _____

6. They won't go swimming. (cold)
    _____

Questions with how often: adverbs of frequency (text, page 88)

M What are your eating habits? Fill in the chart about yourself, using the frequency adverbs *always, often, sometimes, rarely, never.*

> Do you...?
> 1. drink coffee in the morning   _____
> 2. have breakfast   _____
> 3. eat salad with lunch   _____
> 4. eat fruit with each meal   _____
> 5. drink milk once a day   _____
> 6. have dessert after dinner   _____

N About your habits. Use the information from the chart in exercise M to write sentences about yourself. Give additional information when possible.

> **Example**
>
> *I never drink coffee in the morning. I always drink tea.*

1. _____
2. _____
3. _____
4. _____
5. _____
6. _____

Name _____   Date _____

O **Interview.** In this activity, you will interview a classmate or family member about diet and exercise habits. Think of ten things to ask about and write them in the chart under *Activity*. You can ask questions about what a person eats and drinks, if they exercise, if they exercise every day, etc. If you want, you can do this part of the activity with a partner.

When you finish writing the activities, ask your partner questions about each one, starting with *Do you...?* Tell the person to answer with *always, often, sometimes, rarely, never.* When possible, ask other questions for additional information.

Example
A: Do you eat breakfast every morning?
B: Sometimes. Usually I am too late to eat breakfast.

	Activity	How often	Comments
Example	*Eat breakfast every morning*	*Sometimes*	*Usually is too late to eat*
1.			
2.			
3.			
4.			
5.			
6.			
7.			
8.			
9.			
10.			

P **Summary.** Write a brief summary of your questionnaire and your partner's answers. Give any additional information you found out.

_____

_____

_____

_____

_____

_____

_____

_____

Talking about table items (text, page 94)

A **Word find.** There are twelve table item words hidden in the puzzle below. The words are down and across. Circle the words. Then write the words on the lines.

P	E	P	P	E	R	W	B	D	M
J	A	Q	L	C	U	P	O	H	G
L	G	L	A	S	S	E	W	S	U
W	A	P	S	A	L	T	L	P	N
S	D	L	K	B	F	G	C	O	A
H	I	A	O	F	O	N	B	O	P
A	S	T	P	T	R	P	U	N	K
K	Y	E	L	Q	K	E	X	F	I
E	S	A	U	C	E	R	O	S	N
R	Z	G	J	R	K	N	I	F	E

bowl

_____   _____

_____   _____

_____   _____

_____   _____

_____   _____

B **Different table settings.** In the box below, draw a typical table setting from your native country. Show where the table items go. Then write a short paragraph describing the table setting.

Example

In Japan, we usually use chopsticks. They are usually....

_____

_____

_____

_____

_____

Name _____   Date _____

Making comparisons with *even* (text, page 95)

C **Spelling changes.** Write the comparative form of each adjective, following the spelling rules given on page 95 of your text.

Example	
small	*smaller*

1. cold _____
2. big _____
3. healthy _____
4. sunny _____
5. nice _____
6. hot _____
7. white _____
8. pretty _____
9. heavy _____
10. funny _____

11. late _____
12. friendly _____
13. dirty _____
14. slow _____
15. early _____
16. windy _____
17. easy _____
18. fast _____
19. cloudy _____
20. angry _____

D **Make comparisons.** Make your own comparisons, using the cues given.

Example	
Compare two cities or countries. (cold)	
New York is cold, but Boston is even colder.	

1. Compare two cities or countries. (cold)

_____

2. Compare two towns. (small)

_____

3. Compare two people. (friendly)

_____

4. Compare two months. (sunny)

_____

5. Compare two people. (heavy)

_____

6. Compare two people. (funny)

_____

7. Compare two months. (hot)

_____

8. Compare two actresses. (pretty)

_____

9. Compare two cities. (big)

_____

10. Compare two people. (nice)

_____

Contrast of *some* and *any* *(text, page 96)*

E **Food for a snack.** A snack is something you eat or drink between meals, either in the middle of the morning, in the middle of the afternoon, or late at night. Write a list of things you have in your kitchen or refrigerator that are good to eat or drink for a snack. Be specific.

_____ _____ _____

_____ _____ _____

_____ _____ _____

F **An evening snack.** Imagine that you and a friend are watching a movie at your place. Write a conversation between you and your friend, using as many lines as you need. Offer your friend things to eat and drink. Your friend may also ask you for things, with *Do you have any...?* Other expressions you may use are: *Sorry. I don't have any ...;* *Would you like some...?; Thanks, but I don't like ...; Sure. I love ... .*

YOU: I'm hungry. How about a snack?

FRIEND: Good idea! Do you have _____? I'm really thirsty.

YOU: _____

FRIEND: _____

YOU: _____

FRIEND: _____

YOU: _____

FRIEND: _____

YOU: _____

FRIEND: _____

Name _____ Date _____

Expressions of frequency; questions with *how often* (text, page 97)

G **Health questions.** A nurse is asking you questions about your diet and health. Answer the questions with complete sentences, using expressions of frequency. For example: *every ...; once a ...; ... times a day/week; rarely; never.*

1. NURSE: How often do you drink coffee or tea?

   _____

2. NURSE: How often do you eat a good breakfast?

   _____

3. NURSE: How often do you eat fruit?

   _____

4. NURSE: How often do you exercise?

   _____

5. NURSE: How often do you get sick?

   _____

One / ones; comparatives; *too* (text, page 99)

H **Looking for something better.** Complete the sentences with *too* or the comparative form of an adjective + *one/ones.*

1. At the restaurant, Marie showed the waiter the dirty fork and asked for a _____

   _____ .

2. Tran's boots aren't very warm. He has to buy some _____ _____ .

3. The Thomas' apartment is _____ small, so they are looking for a

   _____ _____ .

4. The new restaurant was _____ expensive, so next time they will go to a

   _____ _____ .

5. Tom thinks his dining room chairs are ugly, so he is looking for some _____

   _____ .

6. The skirt was _____ long, so Susan tried on a _____ _____ .

7. The first movie was _____ early, so they went to a _____

   _____ .

8. The math problem was _____ difficult, so she tried an _____

   _____ .

9. Amanda's bike was _____ slow, so she bought a _____ _____ .

10. After the meeting, Mr. Franco was _____ angry to talk about the problem.

Irregular past tense: *begin, lose, feel, sleep (text, page 99)*

I **Talking about the past.** Answer the following questions about yourself. Answer in complete sentences. Give additional information when possible.

1. When did you begin studying English?

   _____

2. When did your English class begin today?

   _____

3. How did you feel yesterday?

   _____

4. When did you sleep last night? (From what time to what time)

   _____

5. Did you lose anything recently? What?

   _____

J **Mrs. Wong's diet.** Read about Mrs. Wong's diet. Then complete the story using the past tense form of these verbs: *be, begin, buy, feel, give, go, have, lose, sleep.*

   Last year Mrs. Wong decided to lose some weight and start some healthy habits. First, she (1) _____ to the doctor for a checkup. Her doctor (2) _____ her a diet and exercise plan. The first month she (3) _____ seven pounds. She (4) _____ much better and (5) _____ more energy. She (6) _____ better at night, and (7) _____ not tired during the afternoon. She (8) _____ a new bicycle and started to ride it a few times a week. She also (9) _____ to enjoy exercising for the first time in her life.

More comparisons *(text, page 100)*

K **More, please!** Marco needs to gain weight, so he eats a lot at every meal. Look at his typical dinner and write what he eats and drinks. Give quantities: *quart, glass, cup, bowl, slice, piece.*

Example
He drinks a glass of juice.

1. _____
2. _____
3. _____
4. _____
5. _____
6. _____
7. _____

Name _____ Date _____

L **What do you say?** Read the situation below. Then write a conversation, showing how to accept and refuse food in an English-speaking country.

SITUATION: You are at an American friend's house for dinner. Your friend is serving chicken, potatoes, and a very special salad. You like the dinner, but you really don't like any kind of salad. Politely refuse the salad. Later, when it is time for dessert, your friend offers ice cream or chocolate cake. Tell your friend which one you want.

FRIEND: How is the chicken? Do you like it?
YOU: _____ .
FRIEND: _____ some salad?
YOU: _____ .
Later...
FRIEND: Would you like some dessert? There's_____ .
YOU: _____ .
FRIEND: _____ ?
YOU: I'd love some coffee with milk, thanks.

M **What about in your country?** Read the following situation, and write a short conversation.

SITUATION: You are in your native country, and an American friend is at your house for dinner. You are serving a traditional meal, but your friend isn't eating one of the dishes you made. Do you say anything? After dinner you offer a very special dessert, but your friend says he/she is on a diet.
YOU: _____
FRIEND: _____
YOU: _____
FRIEND: _____
Later...
YOU: _____
FRIEND: _____
YOU: _____
FRIEND: _____

N **Compare the cultures.** Think about the similarities and differences between accepting and refusing food in the U.S. and in your native country. Answer the questions, and then talk about your answers with your classmates.

1. Is it polite to refuse food that is offered to you in the U.S.? What about in your native country?
   _____
   _____

2. How are your two conversations in exercises L and M different? How are they the same?
   _____
   _____

3. Do you think it is impolite (not polite) to refuse food that is offered to you? Why?
   _____
   _____

Unit 9 — Another Visit to the Doctor

Talking about illness *(text, page 107)*

A How about you? Answer the questions, using complete sentences.

> **Example**
>
> What do you do to feel better when you are depressed?
> *When I am depressed, I call a friend to feel better.*

1. What do you do to feel better when you are depressed?

   _____

2. Who do you see for a medical examination?

   _____

3. What liquids are good to drink when you have a cold?

   _____

4. What is a normal temperature? What is a fever's temperature?

   _____

5. Name some kinds of pills.

   _____

6. Where does a pharmacist work and what does a pharmacist do?

   _____

Have got / Has got *(text, page 108)*

B **Are you OK?** You call a friend, but your friend doesn't sound very well on the phone. Write conversations, using the picture cues.

Useful expressions:
Are you OK? / You don't sound very well. / We missed you in class yesterday. / What's the matter? / Are you sick? / Why don't you...? / Maybe you should... / You'd better...

> **Example**
>
> A: *Are you OK? You sound sick.*
> B: *I've got the flu.*
> A: *Maybe you should call your doctor.*

Name _____   Date _____

1.

A: _____

B: _____

A: _____

2.

A: _____

B: _____

A: _____

3.

A: _____

B: _____

A: _____

4.

A: _____

B: _____

A: _____

5.

A: _____

B: _____

A: _____

Talking about ability or possibility with *could* *(text, page 109)*

C How is your life different? Think about the differences between what you could and couldn't do as a child and what you can and can't do now. Write down your ideas below.

1. When I was a child, I could...

_____

_____

_____

_____

2. When I was a child, I couldn't...

_____

_____

_____

_____

3. Now, I can...

_____

_____

_____

_____

4. Now, I can't...

_____

_____

_____

_____

D Your life then and now. Use your notes from exercise C. Write sentences about how your life is different.

> **Example**
>
> *When I was a child, I could wake up early every morning, but now I can't. I am too tired.*

1. _____

2. _____

3. _____

4. _____

5. _____

6. _____

7. _____

8. _____

9. _____

10. _____

Irregular past tense: *cost, drink, forget, tell (text, pages 110-111)*

E **Create a story.** Imagine that you had a very bad day. It seemed like everything was wrong. First read all the questions. Then answer the questions about your day. Use your imagination.

1. Yesterday you woke up very late. What time did you wake up?

_____

2. You felt terrible. What was wrong?

_____

3. You didn't have much time for breakfast. You only had time to drink something. What did you drink?

_____

4. You rushed out of the door, and closed it behind you. What did you forget inside?

_____

5. What did you do then?

_____

6. Did you go to school, work, or the doctor's office? Did you take a bus, train, or taxi?

_____

7. The bus/train/taxi fare was very expensive. How much did it cost?

_____

8. Did you have enough money to pay for it? What did you do?

_____

9. When you finally got to school / work / the doctor's office, someone told you some bad news. What did they tell you?

_____

_____

F **Write your story.** Use the information in exercise E to write a story about your day. After you finish, share your paragraph with your classmates.

_____

_____

_____

_____

_____

_____

_____

Present perfect tense of *be* **+ adjective** *(text, page 112)*

G **A letter to a friend.** Write a short letter to a friend. Tell news about yourself and how you have been. Try to answer some of these questions in your letter.

How have you been?
Have you been well or sick lately?
What have you been worried about?
Have you been depressed or happy?
How has the weather been?
How has your English class been?
Have you been busy lately?

At the end of your letter, ask your friend how he or she is doing. You may want to ask your friend a few of the questions below. You can use one of the following endings to your letter: *Your friend, Yours truly, Sincerely, Love.*

Example

Dear Sandra,
    I got your letter last week. Thanks so much. I'm sorry I didn't write last week, but I have been very busy. Last Sunday I...

_____
(today's date)

_____

_____

_____

_____

_____

_____

_____

_____

_____

_____

_____

_____

    _____

    _____

Name _____ Date _____

Make and *keep* (text, page 114)

H **Your turn.** Write sentences, using the cues.

> **Example**
>
> make me angry
> *A difficult math problem makes me angry.*

1. make me angry

   _____

2. make me happy

   _____

3. make me sad

   _____

4. keep me healthy

   _____

5. keep me warm

   _____

6. keep me dry

   _____

7. keep me busy

   _____

8. make me sick

   _____

Making comparisons (text, page 115)

I **How are you different?** Think about yourself five years ago. How are you different? Write about yourself, using the cues.

> **Example**
>
> thin
> *I was thinner five years ago than I am now.* OR
> *I am thinner now than five years ago.*

1. thin

   _____

2. healthy

   _____

3. my English / good

   _____

4. happy

   _____

5. busy

   _____

J Crossword puzzle. Use the clues below to complete the puzzle.

Across

1. The doctor told her to take one ____ three times a day.
5. The opposite of sick is ____ .
6. When you have a cold, you should drink plenty of _____ .
7. She had a bad ____ throat, so she called the doctor.
10. He was very ____ so he stayed home from school.
11. If a person is ____ , he or she feels very unhappy and sad.
13. The opposite of thin is ____ .
14. After she ____ the medicine, she began to feel better.
15. If your head hurts, you have a ____ .

Down

1. If you give a ____ to a pharmacist, he or she will give you some medicine.
2. If you have a bad cold in your chest, you will probably get a ____ .
3. Aspirin and antibiotics are types of ____ .
4. When you have the ____ , you often have a fever and a headache.
8. He went on a ____ to lose weight.
9. If your ear hurts you have an ____ .
12. A ____ is a very high body

Name _____   Date _____

Unit 10	Cristina and Gino Get Married

Describing a wedding *(text, page 120)*

A **A very unusual wedding!** Read the story and answer the questions. Give additional
information when possible.

Useful vocabulary:
justice of the peace = official who can legally perform weddings
wet suit = a body suit made out of rubber material, worn by scuba divers to keep warm
scuba dive = to swim underwater with tanks of oxygen on the back

UNDERWATER ROMANCE LEADS TO MARRIAGE

The young couple held hands while the justice of the peace read the wedding ceremony. They couldn't hear him very well, but they knew what he was saying. It was a small ceremony: only the bride and groom, the best man, the maid of honor, and the justice of the peace. The rest of the wedding party waited for them at the beach. The wedding was happening 20 feet under water, at a coral reef in Florida.

Mary Walters and Steve Wilson met five years ago, while they were taking a scuba diving class. They spent many weekends scuba diving together. And so when they decided to get married, they wanted an underwater wedding. The groom wore a black wet suit and a white tuxedo jacket. The bride wore a white wet suit with a short, white veil. She held a bouquet of shells. The maid of honor wore a pink wet suit, and the best man wore a black tuxedo jacket and a black wet suit. After the ceremony, they returned to the beach to greet the wedding party. They changed into dry clothes for the reception, and then everyone enjoyed delicious food, music, dancing, and volleyball. The bride said, "People think we are crazy, but it was a very romantic and meaningful wedding. No one will forget this day."

1. When did the couple meet? _____

2. Where was the wedding? _____

3. Who was at the underwater wedding?

   _____

4. Where was the rest of the wedding party? _____

5. Did the bride wear a wedding gown? _____

6. Did she wear a veil? _____

7. What did the groom wear? _____

8. Did they wear their wet suits during the reception?

   _____

9. What did people do during the reception?

   _____

10. What do you think about this wedding?

   _____

For + indirect object *(text, page 121)*

B **So many things to do!** Sandra got married last month in a small ceremony at her parents' house. Look at the list of things Sandra had to do to get ready for her wedding. Then write sentences about what she did.

order flowers for bridesmaids

buy thank you gifts for bridesmaids

prepare menu for the cooks

prepare list of guests for parents

buy special gift for husband-to-be

1. *Sandra ordered flowers for the bridesmaids.* _____

2. _____

3. _____

4. _____

5. _____

Questions with *for* + indirect object *(text, page 122)*

C **What's the question?** Read the answer and write a question. Use information from exercise B.

1. A: *What did Sandra* _____ ?

   B: Flowers.

2. A: *Who* _____ ?

   B: For her husband.

3. A: _____ ?

   B: A menu.

4. A: _____ ?

   B: For the bridesmaids.

5. A: _____ ?

   B: A list of guests.

Separable phrasal verbs *(text, pages 122-123)*

D **What happened?** Tell what is happening in each picture. Write each sentence two ways, separating the phrasal verbs in the second sentence.

Example
The waitress is filling up the cup with coffee.
The waitress is filling the cup up with coffee.

1. _____
   _____

2. _____
   _____

3. _____
   _____

4. _____
   _____

5. _____
   _____

6. _____
   _____

7. _____
   _____

8. _____
   _____

9. _____
   _____

10. _____
    _____

Get + adjective *(text, page 125)*
Get + noun *(text, page 126)*

E **What about you?** Answer the questions, using *get* + adjective or *get* + noun. Give additional information when possible.

Example	When do you usually get hungry for lunch?
	I usually get hungry for lunch at about 12:00.

1. When do you usually get hungry for lunch?

    _____

2. When do you get ready to go to school or work?

    _____

3. Do you get a newspaper every day?

    _____

4. Did you get any phone calls yesterday?

    _____

5. When does the weather get hot in your area?

    _____

6. What do you do when you get a headache?

    _____

7. Do you get nervous when you ride a plane or a train?

    _____

8. Do you get worried during a thunderstorm?

    _____

Shopping for household items *(text, page 128)*

F Sale prices! Look at the ad below. Then write each item next to the correct price.

WARNER'S DEPARTMENT STORE HOME SALE — 20-40% OFF.

Large towels 8.99

Sheets 5.99 – 12.99 each

Tablecloths 100% cotton,
   various sizes 14.99 – 19.99

Five-speed blender 24.99

Vases Chinese designs 10.99

Toaster 2 slice 15.99; 4 slices 19.99

Crystal glasses 1.99 each

Casserole dishes 12.99 each

Serving dishes various sizes 6.99 – 12.99

Sale is Wednesday – Saturday. Enter contest to win $100 gift certificate!

Name _____   Date _____

	Item	Price
Example	*towels*	$8.99

1. _____ $1.99 each
2. _____ $14.99 – 19.99
3. _____ $12.99 each
4. _____ $15.99 and 19.99
5. _____ $10.99
6. _____ $24.99
7. _____ $5.99 – 12.99
8. _____ $6.99 – 12.99

G **You won a prize!** You won a $100 gift certificate from Warner's Department Store. That means you get $100 of items free! What would you like? Choose items from the ad above. Make sure the total amount is under $100. Then write about what you would like.

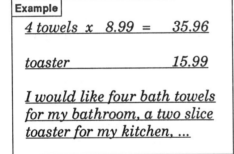

Example

4 towels x 8.99 =   35.96

toaster   15.99

I would like four bath towels for my bathroom, a two slice toaster for my kitchen, ...

List of items and prices

_____

_____

_____

_____

_____

_____

I would like _____

_____

_____

_____

In and *for* *(text, page 129)*

H **Questions of time.** Complete the conversations with *in* or *for*.

1. MARIO: You speak Spanish very well. How long did you live in Mexico?
    TOM: _____ eight months.

2. MRS. SALERNO: When does the flight to Chicago leave?
    AGENT: _____ forty minutes.

3. LISA: I'm so hungry! When is dinner going to be ready?
    PEDRO: _____ ten minutes.

4. MAY: Hi, Sandy.   Do you have a few minutes to talk?
    SANDY: Well, I'm really busy right now. Can I call you back _____ an hour?

5. NGUYEN: When are you going on vacation?
    MARIA: _____ a week.   I'm going to Brazil.
    NGUYEN: That's great. How long will you be there?
    MARIA: _____ ten days.

Final Activity

I **A wedding to remember.** Do you remember a wedding you went to? Write a paragraph describing the wedding. If you don't remember a wedding, create a story about a wedding, using your imagination. Answer some of these questions in your paragraph.

Who were the bride and groom?
Who were the parents of the bride? Of the groom?
When and where was the wedding?
Was the wedding large or small?
What did the bride wear?
Describe the wedding party and the wedding ceremony.
What happened during the reception?
Did you have a good time at the wedding?

_____

_____

_____

_____

_____

_____

_____

_____

_____

Name _____   Date _____

| Unit 11 | Vacation Plans |

Planning a vacation *(text, page 133)*

A **Find a match.** Look at the vocabulary and write each word next to the word or words that are closest in meaning (synonym). You will not use every word.

Vocabulary:
adore / ancient / clear / excitement / luxury / nightlife / romantic / ruins / sandy / spectacular / temple / tropical

Example	
spectacular	great, wonderful

1. _____ full of sand
2. _____ fancy, expensive
3. _____ warm, hot, sunny
4. _____ evening entertainment
5. _____ clean, bright, not cloudy
6. _____ love, like very much
7. _____ fun
8. _____ old, historic

B **Great vacations.** Answer the questions about places to visit, giving complete answers and, when possible, additional information. When you are finished, compare your answers with a classmate.

Example	
What is a spectacular place to visit in your country?	
Niagara Falls is a spectacular place to visit. I went there two years ago.	

1. What is a spectacular place to visit in your country?

   _____

2. Do you know a beach that is famous for its clear, blue water? Where is it?

   _____

3. Name three tropical countries.

   _____

4. What kind of nightlife do you enjoy? Dancing? Music? Theater?

   _____

5. What do you like to do for excitement on vacation? Ski? Hike? Go to new places?

   _____

6. What famous ancient ruins do you know? Where are they?

   _____

7. Is there a luxury hotel in your city or town?

   _____

Talking about future plans *(text, page 134)*

C **Your next vacation.** What are your plans for your next vacation or weekend trip? If you don't have any plans, imagine a trip you would like to take. Answer the questions. Then write a paragraph about your trip, talking about your plans with *going to*.

When are you going to go? _____

Where are you going to go? _____

Who are you planning to go with? _____

How are you going to get there? _____

How long are you going to stay? _____

What are you going to do? _____

_____

_____

_____

_____

_____

_____

_____

_____

Giving additional information *(text, page 134)*

D **Talking about places you know.** Think about five cities in your country or in the world. Write two sentences about each one. In the first sentence, tell where the city is. In the second sentence, tell what the city is famous for.

BOGOTA **ROME** **San Francisco**

PARIS **ATHENΣ** **Barcelona** **LONDON**

Miami

Example
San Francisco is a city that is on the west coast of the United States. *San Francisco is a city that is famous for its hills and trolley cars.*

1. _____

_____

Name _____ Date _____

2. _____

_____

3. _____

_____

4. _____

_____

5. _____

Making comparisons *(text, page 136)*

E **What's your opinion?** Use the cues and give your opinion about people, places, and things.

> **Example**
>
> funny / person / class *Michiko is funnier than any other person in our class.*

1. funny / person / class

_____

2. smart / student / class

_____

3. cold / month / year

_____

4. hot / area / country

_____

5. tall / building / city

_____

6. big / store / city (town)

_____

7. nice / city / world

_____

8. good / TV program / TV

_____

Identifying someone *(text, page 136)*

F **Jobs in the future.** What kinds of jobs will you, your friends, classmates, and family have in the future. Where will they live? Write your predictions for ten people, including yourself. Use your imagination. You can use some of the occupations listed below or others.

Useful vocabulary:

accountant / actor / actress / architect / artist / athlete / clerk / computer programmer / cook / dancer / dentist / doctor / engineer / lawyer / librarian / mechanic / musician / nurse / pharmacist / pilot / police officer / race car driver / salesperson / singer / teacher / writer

Example
My brother Bill will work in Houston as a musician.

1. _____
2. _____
3. _____
4. _____
5. _____
6. _____
7. _____
8. _____
9. _____
10. _____

Irregular past tense: *draw, fall (down), hide, hit, ring, sit (down), tear, write* *(text, page 138)*

G **Things that happened.** Complete the sentences with the past tense forms of these verbs: *draw, fall (down), hide, hit, ring, sit (down), tear, write.*

1. Alesandro _____ the baseball very hard and scored a run for his team.
2. Alice didn't know how to get to Liz's house, so Liz _____ a map.
3. While I was on vacation, I _____ lots of postcards to my friends.
4. The little boy was so angry that he _____ his picture into pieces.
5. While Becky was playing soccer yesterday, she _____ and hurt her knee.
6. Mrs. Norton _____ her husband's birthday present in her closet so he couldn't find it.
7. The schoolchildren got on the bus and _____ in a seat right away.
8. When the bell _____ , all of the students got up and left.

Name _____ Date _____

Final Activities

H **A class trip.** Imagine that your English class won a free class trip to any city in the United States or England. The trip will be five days. Plan your trip, using the questions below as a guide. If possible, work with a partner or in a small group.

1. Where would you like to go?
   _____

2. What is this place famous for?
   _____

3. How will you get there?
   _____

4. Will you stay in a luxury hotel?
   _____

5. What kinds of things will you see?
   _____

6. Will you visit museums / historic buildings / parks / etc.?
   _____

7. What kinds of nightlife will your class enjoy?
   _____

I **Write about your plans.** Now write a paragraph about your class trip, using information from the questions above, and any additional information you can add. Be sure to tell about the city and what it is famous for. For example, *Boston is a city that is famous for its historic buildings.* When you are finished with your paragraph, have a classmate read it. Can he or she help you make it better?

_____

_____

_____

_____

_____

_____

_____

_____

_____

_____

_____

_____

Discussing travel plans *(text, page 145)*

A **What's the best word?** Read each sentence. Find the word or words in the list below that are closest in meaning to the words in *italic*.

conference / elephants / fare / flight / honeymoon / luggage / many plans / protection / round trip / sights / tax / wildlife park

> **Example**
>
> The teachers are attending a *large meeting* in New York City. <u>conference</u>

1. The children were very excited to see the *large gray animals* at the zoo. _____

2. There are many fascinating *places to visit* in Washington, D.C. _____

3. The ticket agent took the *suitcases* at the ticket counter. _____

4. Elinor Young will visit a *special place for animals* in Africa. _____

5. Elinor Young has *a very busy schedule* for her trip. _____

6. The *cost for the ticket* from New York to Miami was $284, *to go and come back.* _____

7. This price includes *an additional charge that is paid to the government.* _____

8. *The airplane trip* takes 2 1/2 hours from New York to Miami. _____

9. Many wild animals in the world need *agencies to help them.* _____

10. Cristina and Gino are planning *a special trip after their wedding.* _____

Talking about plans and intentions *(text, page 145)*

B **Conversation clues.** Read each conversation and complete it with the correct form of one of the verbs listed. Be sure to put the verb in the correct tense. Some items have more than one correct answer.

begin to / decide to / forget to / hope to / need to / plan to / promise to / remember to / start to / try to

1. A: How was your basketball game yesterday?
   B: Not so good. We were walking to the tennis courts when it _____ rain.
2. A: I'm going to the store because I _____ buy some milk.
   B: Oh. Don't _____ get some bread, too.
3. A: What movie are you and Tim going to see tonight?
   B: We _____ see the new Tom Cruise movie. I hope it's good.
4. A: And _____ take your medicine before each meal.
   B: Yes, Dr. Young. I won't forget.

5. A: I don't know what's wrong with my car. I _____ start it, but nothing happened.

   B: Call the mechanic at the Main Street gas station. Maybe he can help you.

6. A: What are you going to do after you graduate from college?

   B: I _____ get a job in an advertising company.

7. A: What did you think about that problem in math class?

   B: Well, I think I _____ understand it now. Let me show you.

8. A: What are you going to do during your vacation?

   B: I _____ visit my aunt and uncle, and then see my grandparents.

9. A: Why didn't you call me last night? You _____ call me after work!

   B: I'm really sorry. I got home from work very late, and I thought it was too late to call.

Talking about the future *(text, page 146)*

C **A free trip!** Imagine you won a free trip to England or the United States. You will spend one week in the country. You can invite one person. Plan your trip by giving short answers to the questions.

1. Will you go to England or the United States? _____

2. Who will you invite to go with you? A relative? A friend? _____

3. Will you take a lot of luggage or just one suitcase? _____

4. Will you visit the typical tourist sights or the unusual places?

   _____

5. Will you stay in big luxury hotels? _____

6. What will you see on your trip? _____

   _____

D **Your trip plans.** Write a paragraph about your trip, using information from exercise C. Add more information and details about your trip. Here are some words you can use:

buy / pack / visit / hope to / plan to / sights / historical / ancient / museums / parks

_____

_____

_____

_____

_____

_____

_____

Correcting information *(text, page 147)*

E **John's vacation.** Next week is John's vacation and he's thinking about his plans. Read the statements below and say if they are correct or incorrect. If a statement is incorrect, give the correct information.

> **Example**
>
> John is going on vacation next week.
> *That's right.*
> John is depressed about his plans.
> *No, he isn't. He's very excited about his plans.*

1. John is going to go with his wife.

   _____

2. They will go skiing in the mountains.

   _____

3. He will relax and read.

   _____

4. He plans to play some volleyball.

   _____

5. They are going to go dancing at night.

   _____

6. They will swim every day.

   _____

7. John will visit some big cities.

   _____

8. They hope to ride motorcycles.

   _____

9. John is going to buy some sandals as souvenirs.

   _____

10. They are going to have a terrible time.

    _____

Asking for information *(text, page 148)*

F **An imaginary trip.** Imagine that you won a free one-week trip to another country. Think for a minute about where you would like to go and what you would like to do. Then with a partner ask each other about your trips. Use the cues below to write questions. Ask your partner the questions and write down the answers.

> **Example**
> Where / go / trip   A: *Where will you go on your trip?*
>   B: *I'll go to England.*

1. Where / go / trip   A: _____
                          B: _____

2. Who / go / you   A: _____
                          B: _____

3. What / take / you   A: _____
                          B: _____

4. What / do / there   A: _____
                          B: _____

5. What kind / sights / see   A: _____
                          B: _____

To + indirect object *(text, page 150)*

G **What's happening?** Describe what's happening in each picture, using the cues given. Use these verbs + *to* + indirect object: give / read / sell / send / show / teach / write.

> **Example**
> Mary / her sister   *Mary is giving a cup of coffee to her sister.*

1. _____
   Julio / Tom

2. _____
   Victor / Alice

3.  _____
   Julie / her mother

4.  _____
   Sheila / her friend

5.  _____
   Shinya / his brother

Indirect and direct objects *(text, page 151)*

H **Scrambled sentences.** Put the words in the correct order to form a sentence.
CLUE: the first word in the sentence starts with a capital letter.

> **Example**
>
> visitors / some / We / our / coffee / are / for / making
> *We are making some coffee for our visitors.*

1. birthday / I'm / a / to / my / buy / for / going / present / sister

_____

2. some / He / to / his / has / brother / money / send / to

_____

3. a / her / new / got / Martha / watch / mother

_____

4. rarely / The / wrote / parents / boy / his / to

_____

5. a / story / before / bedtime / Alicia / reads / her / son

_____

6. is / to / He / to / his / sell / going / uncle / car / his

_____

7. wonderful / gave / My / a / me / cookbook / friend

_____

8. his / Rick / next / show / friends / new / will / car / his / weekend

_____

9. a / gave / graduation / their / The / Wilsons / son / party

_____

10. cost / This / about / me / book / $20

_____

I **Questions for you.** Answer the questions, using complete sentences.

1. Who is teaching you English?

_____

2. Who sometimes sends you a package?

_____

3. Who do you sometimes write a letter to?

_____

4. Do you need to buy something for someone? Tell who and what.

_____

5. Who read books to you when you were young?

_____

Name _____   Date _____

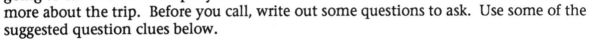

Final Activities

J   **A Vermont bike trip.** If possible, do this
activity with a partner. Read the roles
below, and choose one. Then do a role
play with your partner.

Role A. You want to go on a bike trip in
Vermont. You saw an ad in the newspaper for a three-day bike trip. You are
going to call the tour company to ask
more about the trip. Before you call, write out some questions to ask. Use some of the
suggested question clues below.

What / Where / How long / What do I need to / When / How much / How many / Is there
(NOTE: Don't look on page 78.)

_____

_____

_____

_____

_____

Role B. You are a tour guide with Vermont Bike Tours. Read the advertisement below
and the itineraries on page 78. Then answer your partner's questions.

Want to see the best of Vermont?
Bike it! with
Vermont Bike Tours

   Our professional bike tour guides can show you the Vermont that most tourists never
see. From a bike, you won't miss any of the beautiful sights: mountains, rivers, covered
bridges, wildlife, flowers, small towns, farms, country stores. Each day, our truck will carry
your luggage to our next destination, usually a country inn in a small town. You just have
to ride your bike and enjoy Vermont.
   Trips are two days and three days. Trips for teens or adults. Reasonable rates! Call
today for more information and a brochure.

INFORMATION ON 2-DAY AND 3-DAY BIKE TRIPS

Trip 1 Brandon to Fort Ticonderoga, 44 miles
Trip one starts in Brandon. There is a small museum there. We ride to Shoreham, and visit art galleries. We ride through many apple orchards and by many dairy farms. We will take a ferry boat across Lake Champlain. We will vist Fort Ticonderoga, a famous military fort from the American Revolution. Cost: $150, one night.

Trip 2 Middlebury to Vergennes, 51 miles
Trip 2 starts in the college town of Middlebury. We will stay in the historic Middlebury Inn. In Middlebury, we will tour the Sheldon Museum, which has exhibits of early New England life. We will also tour Middlebury College, a small liberal arts school. We will ride along Lake Champlain, see several important Revolutionary War sites, swim in the lake, and visit an apple orchard, and ride through a covered bridge. We will finish at the University of Vermont Morgan Horse Farm, with a tour of the historic farm. Cost: $200, two nights.

Trip 3 Arlington to North Bennington, 47 miles
Trip 3 features beautiful Southwestern Vermont. We will ride through a covered bridge, see where artist Norman Rockwell lived, tour a pottery studio, swim in a sparkling river, and visit several small museums. This ride features many scenic views of Vermont countryside. Cost: $150, one night.

Things to bring: bike, bike helmet (hat), sun glasses, clothes, swimming suit, raincoat, sweater, scarf, water bottle, camera.

K **Write it out.** After you practice the role play in exercise J with your partner, write out the conversation.

B: Vermont Bike Tours. May I help you?

A: _____

B: _____

A: _____

B: _____

A: _____

B: _____

A: _____

B: _____

A: _____

B: _____

A: _____

B: _____

Unit 13 | On the Way

Expressing an additional negative statement *(text, page 157)*

A **Interviews.** In this activity, you need to find two people to answer *no* to each question. First, write questions to ask your classmates or friends, using the cues. For number 10, make up your own question. Then ask your classmates or friends the questions. When a person answers negatively, write his or her name under the question.

> **Example**
>
> Can you speak *Arabic?*
> No: *Tran* *Jose*

1. Can you speak _____ ?

   No: _____ _____

2. Do you like to _____ ?

   No: _____ _____

3. Did you _____ last night?

   No: _____ _____

4. Were you _____ yesterday?

   No: _____ _____

5. Can you _____ well?

   No: _____ _____

6. Are you _____ ?

   No: _____ _____

7. Do you _____ every day?

   No: _____ _____

8. Did you _____ yesterday?

   No: _____ _____

9. Do you _____ ?

   No: _____ _____

10. _____

   No: _____ _____

B **And he/she doesn't either.** Use the information from exercise A to write sentences about your classmates or friends using *either*.

> **Example**
>
> *Tran can't speak Arabic, and Jose can't either.*

1. _____
2. _____
3. _____
4. _____
5. _____
6. _____
7. _____
8. _____
9. _____
10. _____

Talking about things that are about to happen *(text, page 158)*

C **What's about to happen?** Describe what is about to happen in each picture.

> **Example**
>
> *He is about to eat a sandwich.*

1. _____ 2. _____

3. _____ 4. _____

Name _____ Date _____

5. _____   6. _____

7. _____   8. _____

Contrasting *a little* and *a few* (text, page 159)

D **What's in the refrigerator?** Pierre doesn't have much in his refrigerator. Describe what's in his refrigerator, using *a little* and *a few*.

> **Example**
>
> *He has a few eggs.*

1. _____

2. _____

3. _____

4. _____

5. _____

6. _____

7. _____

8. _____

9. _____

10. _____

Much, many, and a lot of (text, page 160)

E **Your city or town.** Imagine that a tourist wants to visit your city or town. The tourist has many questions to ask you. Write the tourist's questions, using the cues and *much* or *many*. Then answer the questions with *many / not much / not many / a lot of*.

> **Example**
>
> theaters   A: *Are there many theaters in your city?*
>
> B: *Yes, there are many theaters.* OR
>
> *No, there aren't many theaters.* OR
>
> *No, there aren't any theaters.*

1. luxury hotels   A: _____

   B: _____

2. tourist sights   A: _____

   B: _____

3. public transportation   A: _____

   B: _____

4. parks   A: _____

   B: _____

5. museums   A: _____

   B: _____

6. pollution   A: _____

   B: _____

7. historic buildings A: _____

   B: _____

8. crime   A: _____

   B: _____

9. night entertainment A: _____

   B: _____

F **Conversations to finish.** Complete the conversations with *much, many,* or *a lot of.*

1. A: Do you want to go to a movie tonight?
   B: I'd love to go, but I have _____ homework to do.

2. A: How _____ sugar do you like in your coffee?
   B: Just a little, thanks.

3. A: I have so _____ to read for tomorrow's class!
   B: Really? How _____ pages do you have to read?
   A: About fifty pages.
   B: Wow! That's _____ homework.

4. A: Did you buy _____ souvenirs on your trip?
   B: Yes, I bought _____ souvenirs. In fact, I had to buy another suitcase to pack them in.

Final Activity

G **Great places to visit.** Write a paragraph about a great place to visit. It should be a place you know about. Give as much information as possible about the city or place. Tell what the place is famous for, what there is to see, fun things to do, places to eat or visit, etc. First write some notes to organize your thoughts. Then write your paragraph. After you finish, share your paragraph with a partner. Can he or she help you make it better?

NOTES: Place: _____

_____

_____

_____

_____

Paragraph

_____

_____

_____

_____

_____

_____

_____

_____

Unit 14	**Away from Home**

Talking about plans *(text, page 167)*

A **What's the definition?** Match the following words with the correct definition.

lecture / market / natural / protect / surprise / surprised / surroundings / tour / zoo

1. _____ : a place where a collection of wild animals is kept for public showing
2. _____ : amazed, astonished
3. _____ : an informative talk to a class or group
4. _____ : a gathering of people for buying and selling goods
5. _____ : a long trip, as for sightseeing
6. _____ : something that amazes or astonishes
7. _____ : the things, conditions, etc., around a person, animal, or thing
8. _____ : to shield or defend from injury, danger
9. _____ : true to nature, not artificial

B **Use the words.** Choose five words listed above. Write your own sentences with them.

1. _____
2. _____
3. _____
4. _____
5. _____

Asking about possession *(text, page 167)*

C **Whose is it?** Look at the picture and write the question or the answer.

Example
A: Whose dog is that?
B: *It's Donna's.*

Brian   Donna   Sandra   Kim   Linda   Mike   Mr. Block

1. A: Whose earrings are those?
   B: _____

2. A: Whose coffee is that?
   B: _____

3. A: _____
   B: They're Brian's.

4. A: Whose shoes are those?
   B: _____

5. A: _____
   B: They're Mr. Brock's.

6. A: Whose hat is that?
   B: _____

84 Unit Fourteen

Name _____   Date _____

Making comparisons *(text, page 169)*

D **What's your opinion?** Compare two people or things, using the cues given. Use *more ... than* or *less... than*.

> **Example**
>
> Compare two men. (handsome)
> *Ken is more handsome than Charles.*

1. Compare two restaurants. (expensive)

   _____

2. Compare two movies. (exciting)

   _____

3. Compare two people. (famous)

   _____

4. Compare two cities. (crowded)

   _____

5. Compare two singers. (talented)

   _____

6. Compare two places to visit. (spectacular)

   _____

7. Compare two people. (nervous)

   _____

8. Compare two tourist sights. (unusual)

   _____

9. Compare two parks. (beautiful)

   _____

10. Compare two hotels. (modern)

   _____

Agreeing with a negative statement *(text, page 170)*

E **So much in common!** Rosa wants to introduce her friend Marie to Mark. Marie is very shy, and doesn't want to meet Mark. She makes up excuses, but each time Rosa says that Mark feels the same way. Complete the conversation, using *neither*.

ROSA: Marie, I really think that you'll like Mark. He's so friendly!

MARIE: But I don't like to meet new people!

ROSA: That's OK. *Neither does Mark*. But you have to. He's going to meet us at House of Pizza at 7:00.

MARIE: But I don't like pizza!

ROSA: That's funny. _____. Well, maybe we should meet at the Mexican restaurant instead.

MARIE: That's better than the pizza place. But I never know what to say.

ROSA: Don't worry, _____ . But after he gets to know you, you'll both have a lot to talk about.

MARIE: Oh, really? Like what?

ROSA: Well, tennis.

MARIE: But I can't play tennis.

ROSA: I know. _____. But he wants to learn, and I know you do, too. And math class. You are both in the same math class.

MARIE: I know. But I'm not a good math student and _____ .

ROSA: But Mark's brother is an excellent math student, and he could help both of you. Come on! Don't be so shy. It'll be fun.

MARIE: Well, I guess I'll go with you to meet him. I didn't make any other plans for tonight.

ROSA: Great! _____. Let's go. He can't wait for you two to meet.

MARIE: Actually, _____.

Talking about past events *(text, page 171)*

F **A weekend trip.** Complete the paragraph using the correct form of *spend, cost,* and *pay*.

Pedro took a weekend trip to see his friend John. Pedro is a student, so he doesn't have much money and doesn't like to (1) _____ too much on the weekend. He thought he would need about $50, but in the end he (2) _____ about $60. The gas for his car (3) _____ about $20, round trip. When he got to John's house, he saw that John didn't have a very big kitchen or refrigerator. Also, John hates to cook. So, they ate lunch and dinner in restaurants, and Pedro had to (4) _____ money on meals. On Saturday night they went to a movie, and Pedro (5) _____ for both tickets. By Sunday afternoon, Pedro didn't have much money left, so John (6) _____ for the Science Museum tickets. They had a good time and enjoyed the weekend, but Pedro (7) _____ too much money. He thought, "Next weekend I'll stay home and it won't (8) _____ me anything!"

Forming nouns from verb + *-tion*   *(text, page 172)*

G **Word forms.** Complete the columns with the missing noun or verb.

Verb	Noun
1. *describe*	description
2. _____	introduction
3. translate	_____
4. converse	_____
5. _____	protection
6. contribute	_____
7. act	_____
8. _____	preparation
9. celebrate	_____
10. _____	donation
11. inform	_____
12. _____	exhibition
13. invite	_____
14. locate	_____

H **What's the word?** Use words from exercise G to complete the sentences. Change the form of the words as needed (verb tense, singular - plural).

1. Mrs. Clark _____ a wonderful meal yesterday. The _____ took about three hours.

2. It is important to _____ young children from accidents.

3. Last year there was a big _____ for her grandmother's 90th birthday.

4. Yesterday we received an _____ to go to my cousin's wedding in June.

5. The new apartment has a very good _____ . It's near public transportation and a shopping mall.

6. My uncle is a professor of Spanish.   In addition to teaching, he sometimes _____ books from English to Spanish.

7. Last year the artist _____ his paintings in several cities.

8. The _____ of the trip in the brochure was very interesting and informative.

9. The soccer coach asked each player to make a _____ of $10 for the uniforms.

10. Yesterday my friend _____ me to a new student from Portugal.

Making a choice *(text, page 173)*

I **Which one?** Use the cues to ask and answer questions with *which*.

> **Example**
>
> Compare two department stores.   (larger)
> A: *Which store is larger: White's or MacGovern's?*
> B: *MacGovern's* .

1. Compare two department stores. (more expensive)

   A: _____

   B: _____

2. Compare two countries. (more beautiful)

   A: _____

   B: _____

3. Compare two buildings. (more modern)

   A: _____

   B: _____

4. Compare two tourist sights. (more spectacular)

   A: _____

   B: _____

5. Compare two restaurants. (better)

   A: _____

   B: _____

Talking about shopping *(text, page 174)*

J **On sale!** Complete the sentences with *for sale, sale, on sale, sell,* or *sold.*

1. Jim wants to _____ his car, so he put a sign in the window that says

   _____ .

2. Trisha and Kim are going shopping tomorrow because there's a big

   _____ at Warner's Department store.

3. The shoes weren't very expensive because they were _____ .

4. The Smiths' house is _____ because they are going to move to
   California.

5. If you look carefully, you will always find something _____ in each
   department of a large store.

6. Joan needs a new coat. She doesn't have much money. She's going to go to a store
   that's having a _____ on coats.

7. My brother _____ his old car for $800.

8. They _____ all different kinds of international foods in that
   supermarket.

Irregular past tense: *blow, cut, light, put, sing, teach* (text, page 175)

K **What happened?** Complete the sentences with the correct past tense form of these verbs: *blow, cut, light, put, sing, teach.*

1. At her birthday party, after they _____ "Happy Birthday," Molly

   _____ out the candles.

2. Yesterday, Alice _____ her finger while she was making dinner.

3. Last summer I _____ my younger sister how to swim.

4. After we _____ the fire in the living room, it was very warm.

5. The children _____ their favorite songs while their mother drove them in

   the car.

6. It was so windy yesterday that it _____ over several chairs in the yard.

7. Mr. Gomez _____ math for 20 years before he retired.

8. Tomas _____ the juice on the table and then poured some for each person.

Final Activity

L **A fun shopping trip.** Do you like to shop? Everyone has to shop sometime, like it or not. In this activity, imagine that you went on a fun shopping trip. You had lots of money to spend, you found what you needed, everything was on sale, and you had a great time. Write a story about your trip, telling what happened. Use your imagination! Before you write, think about answers to these questions.

Where did you go shopping?   How much did things cost?
Who went with you?   What did you do that was fun?
What did you buy? Describe   Did anything unusual happen?
   each thing and why you bought it.

_____

_____

_____

_____

_____

_____

_____

After you finish your story, share it with a partner. Can he or she make any suggestions to improve it?